G000276049

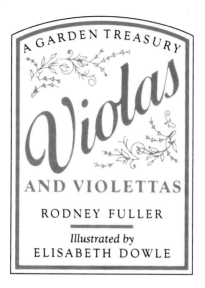

A GARDEN TREASURY

Violas

AND VIOLETTAS

RODNEY FULLER

Illustrated by
ELISABETH DOWLE

HarperCollins*Publishers*

First published in 1994 by
HarperCollins Publishers, London

Created exclusively for HarperCollins by Clare Clements

Designer: Clare Clements
Editor: Caroline Taylor

For HarperCollins Publishers
Commissioning Editor: Polly Powell
Project Editor: Barbara Dixon

A CIP catalogue record for this book is available
from the British Library

ISBN 0 00 412959 8

Typeset in WTC Goudy by SX Composing Ltd
Colour reproduction in Singapore by Colourscan
Printed and bound in Italy

'The power to lighten our cares and carry
ease to our hearts still lies in this lowly, yet lovely flower.'
JAMES SIMKINS, 1889

ACKNOWLEDGEMENTS

Clare Clements would like to thank Nigel and Aaron,
and Elisabeth Dowle would like to thank John and
Matthew for their encouragement and support during
the preparation of this book.

Contents

Introduction

The question most frequently asked is, 'What is the difference between a viola and a violetta?' – and it is not easy to provide a precise answer without offering a brief explanation of the historical origins of each.

THE VIOLA

There will always be a degree of confusion relating to the name 'viola' as applied to hybrid garden violas because, to a botanist, *Viola* is also the correct name for the entire genus, which encompasses all the countless species, subspecies and varieties of pansies, violas, violettas and violets. A century ago strenuous efforts were made by William Robinson, proprietor and editor of *The Garden*, to persuade nurserymen and gardeners to adopt the name 'tufted pansy' instead, but to no avail, and 'viola' has remained the universally accepted name to this day.

It all began in the 1860s with experimental cross breeding between existing garden pansies and other wild species of viola, notably *V. lutea* and *V. cornuta*, the latter a hardy perennial species from the Pyrenees, which had been introduced to Britain almost a hundred years earlier. The flowers of *V. cornuta* have narrow, relatively undeveloped petals, which give them an attractively light and delicate appearance, and the plant has a particularly vigorous root system which spreads by the formation of underground

Princess Mab, a violetta with textured flowers

rooting stems or stolons. These can be detached when sufficiently developed, and used for propagation. Cross-fertil-
ization with the garden pansy gave rise to a small number of
plants which inherited the considerably more compact,
branched and tufted habit of *V. cornuta*. These plants were
also more perennial in nature, were easier to cultivate, and
had a significantly extended flowering season. Their introduction was greeted with considerable enthusiasm.

THE VIOLETTA

By the mid 1870s interest began to develop in the viola's
habit of growth. This was soon considered to be of greater
importance than the size of the flowers alone, which had,
until that time, been the overriding obsession. Greater
emphasis began to be placed upon the viola's profusion
and continuity of flowering and on its more compact and
tufted habit.

The superior garden merit of these comparatively
miniature varieties was soon recognized, and by 1887 the
Scottish pioneer Dr Charles Stuart had introduced a particularly fine pure white variety, which was not only totally
devoid of the characteristic rays or whiskers, but also had
an especially fine fragrance. He named this variety
'Violetta'. Further breeding resulted in an extended colour
range of plants which were all similar in habit, and could
thus be identified as a distinct strain of viola, to which was
given the name violetta.

At the Viola Conference held at Birmingham in 1894, it
was decided that, in order to provide a basis of set

*Moonlight, a hardy viola with delicate,
dainty, long-stemmed flowers*

standards upon which growers could
compete against one another at the
flower shows, the time had come to
publish an official definition of the essential requirements for a violetta. The basic
rules agreed upon determined that the
flowers should be no less than 1 in/2.5 cm,
and no more than 1½ in/3 cm in width; that
they should be distinctly fragrant; without
rays; freely produced on erect stems; and that the
plants should have small neat foliage and be of
dwarf, bushy, tufted habit. However, in response to
criticism of what were considered to be unduly re-
stricting rules regarding the size of the flowers, the
British Viola and Pansy Floral Committee, a con-
sortium of seven regional Pansy and Viola Societies,
subsequently decreed that the size of the flowers
should be no less than ½ in/1.25 cm, and no more than
1 in/2.5 cm in width, thereby opening the way for many fine,
smaller-flowered but equally attractive varieties which had
hitherto been excluded on size alone.

Today there is little or no competitive showing of violettas
in the traditional manner, and plants with flowers that fall
into both categories are now offered for sale. In theory this
still precludes a variety which lacks distinct fragrance, and it
is perhaps a mistake to be too dogmatic in such matters.

In view of all their admirable qualities, it is surprising that violas and violettas are not cultivated in our gardens today to the same extent as the ubiquitous pansy. The viola and violetta undoubtedly shared equal glory with the pansy throughout the early years of this century, but fashion dictates, and a decline in interest had the inevitable result that many fine varieties slipped into extinction. It is only in the last twenty years or so that a few dedicated enthusiasts have successfully rekindled interest in violas and violettas by seeking out, propagating and distributing those that have survived, and by introducing fresh new varieties.

CULTIVATION

The violas and violettas of today are amongst the most rewarding of all flowering plants. They flower continuously from spring until the first frost of autumn; their cultivation requires no particular soil or exceptional skill; and they are remarkably resistant to pests and diseases. They flower best when grown in cool moist soil fully exposed to the summer sun. They will not, however, perform well if the soil becomes too hot and dry for any length of time, and so it is perhaps

Magenta Maid, a floriferous viola of dwarf, vigorous, tufted habit

advisable to choose a spot where the plants will have protection from direct sunlight for at least part of the day. Heavy shade will inhibit flowering and induce the plants to elongate in search of sunlight. Violas and violettas, particularly those of more elusive and subtle colouring, show themselves at their best in soft gentle summer twilight.

Young plants should be planted into their flowering quarters in spring. They can be expected to commence flowering in April, and by midsummer a young plant should have developed into a fine specimen 10 in/25 cm or more in diameter, smothered in blossom.

Unless it is the intention to harvest the seed, it is advisable to remove fading flowers in order that energy which would be expended on seed formation is diverted into the production of more flowers. As the season progresses the flowers will gradually diminish in size, but they will be borne in such profusion that this is of little consequence. Slugs and snails should be discouraged as they may disfigure the flowers by nibbling the petals. If the plants become lank and untidy they can be rejuvenated by trimming back the longer growths to encourage fresh basal shoots. If the roots are kept moist and the soil free of weeds all should be well.

PROPAGATION

Seedlings of hybrid violas and violettas seldom come true to type and are almost invariably of inferior quality to the parent plants. The only satisfactory way to propagate named hybrid varieties is to divide a mature plant or preferably take cuttings of healthy young basal growth.

Johnny Jump Up

◁ The name 'Johnny Jump Up' is the name adopted in the United States of America for this selected garden form of the small-flowered wild species, *V. tricolor*. The British favour the name 'Heartsease'. *V. tricolor* is the most significant ancestor from which so many of the larger-flowered and more flamboyant hybrid garden pansies and violas are descended. The charming little elongated flowers in combinations of varying shades of yellow, violet and mauve set seed readily, to provide each succeeding season's crop of plants. Self-sown seedlings are a feature of a true cottage garden.

Purple Dove

▷ The robust foliage and tall, rather lax habit of growth of this viola leave little doubt as to its pansy parentage. The flowers are comparatively large. The two upper petals are of rich purple, the two middle petals cream with a delicate flecking of purple around their outer margins, and the lower petal is of a richer yellow with similar splashes of purple. For maximum dramatic effect this variety is best planted in groups of three, five or preferably more. As each plant matures it will intermingle with its neighbour, and in so doing provide a mass of self-supporting blossom.

V. cornuta 'Alba'

▷ This pure white variety of the
species *V. cornuta* possesses the
hardy perennial qualities which are
common to all the cornuta violas. It is
ideal for planting in an informal mixed her-
baceous border, where it will scramble
upwards, using taller plants for support,
often attaining considerable height. *V. cornuta* 'Alba' blooms for weeks on end throughout the summer, and can be expected to pro-
duce worthwhile self-sown seedlings when permitted to do
so. The best of these can be vegetatively propagated.

Julian

◁ A splendid little viola, worthy of a place in any collection,
'Julian' was introduced by the highly respected Lancashire
nurseryman, Reginald Kaye. Reliably hardy, compact and ex-
tremely floriferous, the comparatively small short-stemmed
flowers have slightly frilled petals of a delicate but positive
warm sky blue. 'Julian' flowers with such profusion as to virtually obscure from view its entire foliage. Its tidy dwarf
habit of growth makes for a fine plant for edging a formal
border or path. It is equally suitable for growing in cool moist
soil in a pot, tub, trough or window box. Removal of fading
flowers will encourage further flower buds.

Mrs Chichester

▷ This large-flowered viola is one of the older varieties whose vigour has ensured that it survived the test of time. The petals are basically white, dramatically overlaid with violet-purple streaks. Pronounced rays radiate from the rich yellow centre of the flower. 'Mrs Chichester' is suitable for the larger scale of bedding and border schemes, and its size and substance also make it a suitable variety to consider for cutting so that it can be used in floral decorations.

Magic

◁ This variety of V. *gracilis* is of graceful and deceptively delicate appearance. The heavily rayed flowers have the intriguing characteristic of changing colour throughout the season. Early season flowers are the typical violet colour of the species but, as the summer progresses, subsequent flowers are paler in colour and ultimately become all but white. This may appear to be a magical transformation, but it is in fact an indication that the pigment in the flower is unable to survive the bleaching effect of hot midsummer sunshine. This variety is more an object of fascination than a flamboyant performer.

Thalia

▷ This particularly attractive violetta has small, slightly elongated flowers of rich cream, the upper petals being suffused and edged with soft mauve. Somewhat concave petals, like little ears, never open entirely flat as in other varieties, and this contributes greatly to its individual character and charm. Abundant flowers on rigid stalks crowning a compact cushion of bright foliage combine to make a perfect little specimen plant for a small border, tub, trough or window box.

Primrose Dame

◁ This appropriately named, old-established, traditional-style bedding viola has moderately large flowers of pure pale primrose yellow with a neat central orange eye. It is appreciated to best effect when planted in informal drifts, and its soft gentle dignity is a contrast to the more vivid and dramatic colours of the flower garden. The flowers are of fine substance on strong stems, and if cut and immediately placed in a vase of water are ideal for small-scale table decoration. If protected from direct sunlight they should remain fresh for two or three days. Alternatively, the flower heads can be preserved in a flower press and used for a variety of artistic purposes.

V. cornuta 'Rosea'

◁ A good cornuta variety of recent introduction with small well-developed petals of warm glowing rosy purple. It is an easy, most reliable and rewarding plant, smothered with blossom for week after week throughout the summer months. It has the typical vigour and habit of the cornutas and is suitable for mass planting to form a carpet beneath deciduous shrubs and trees, although excessive shade will inhibit flowering. The variety V. cornuta 'Seymour Pink' with its pink, white-centred flowers is an ideal and equally vigorous companion or alternative to V. cornuta 'Rosea'.

James Pilling

▷ A large robust flower of fine substance, and a suitable variety to be cultivated by those who aspire to exhibit and show the flowers competitively in the traditional manner. The flowers, which are circular in outline, have a wide outer margin of rich violet-mauve which gradually reduces in strength to a white centre, and are held proudly aloft on rigid stems; characteristics which render staging as a formal display on the show bench so much more satisfactory. 'James Pilling' is a good old-established variety of classic proportions, which must never be permitted to slip into extinction.

Aspasia

▷ A vigorous viola with very compact tufted growth crowned by a mass of small elongated flowers, of which the two top petals are cream and the lower petals a deep golden yellow. Raised in recent years by Richard Cawthorne, it received the Royal Horticultural Society's Award of Merit in 1981. It is a fine variety for those who prefer the small or miniature-flowered violas. For general cultivation it is these varieties which are particularly floriferous, robust and wind resistant. After flowering is over, there remains a cushion of neat ever-green foliage which can benefit from being transplanted into fresh ground.

Molly Sanderson

◁ Introduced in recent years, this viola soon became a firm favourite. The plant is of neat compact habit and blooms freely. The petals of the dainty flowers are rich velvety black. Raised in Kent by Dr Scott Stone, nurtured and propagated in Northern Ireland by Dr Molly Sanderson, and subsequently attracting the attention of Ralph Haywood of the Royal Horticultural Society, this distinctive variety is, without a doubt, here to stay. It is best grown in semi-shade to prevent the petals from flagging in the heat of the sun.

V. cornuta 'Belmont Blue' and 'Boughton Blue'

◁ Of these two virtually indistinguishable cornuta varieties, 'Boughton Blue' has slightly greater strength of colour and more pronounced rays. The flowers of both are of soft pale sky blue with a mere hint of lilac to add a touch of warmth. These are ideal varieties to use as ground-cover beneath roses or other deciduous shrubs which will allow sufficient sunshine to filter through. They should rapidly form an impenetrable carpet of blossom in the summer.

Maggie Mott

▷ The legendary 'Maggie Mott' has for many years held a particular place in the affections of all viola lovers. This particularly fine large-flowered and superbly fragrant silvery mauve cream-centred viola was raised by Mr F. Burdett, gardener to Mr Albert Mott of Sunningdale, Berkshire, and exhibited at the Royal Horticultural Society in 1902 and 1912. 'Maggie Mott' was named after Mr Mott's eldest daughter, who died in 1958 at the age of ninety. It received the Royal Horticultural Society's coveted Award of Merit in 1922, and has remained a firm favourite to this day.

Vita

◁ This attractive viola is believed to have originated in the gardens of Sissinghurst Castle in Kent, the former home of the eminent gardeners Victoria (Vita) Sackville-West and Harold Nicolson. The small flowers are dainty and delicate in texture; all petals are of an unusual, slightly flecked soft lavender-pink with a small neat eye of cream. The plant has a somewhat lax habit of growth and is best planted near to the front of the flower border or in a moist pocket of the rock garden where it can be isolated from invasion by more boisterous neighbouring plants.

Haslemere

▷ No collection of the smaller-flowered violas should be deemed to be complete without the inclusion of this exceptional variety (syn. 'Nellie Britton'). The flowers are a most attractive and unusual shade of soft dusky lilac-pink. Raised in the nurseries of seed merchants Thompson and Morgan, 'Haslemere' earned them the Royal Horticultural Society's Award of Merit when exhibited in 1923. Devon nurserywoman Miss Nellie Britton subsequently played a vital role in ensuring the survival and distribution of this most distinctive variety.

Leora

◁ This little violetta is one of numerous fine varieties raised and introduced in recent years by Mr Richard Cawthorne. It fulfils the majority of the essential qualities of a violetta as originally defined. The small rich yellow and slightly elongated fragrant flowers are displayed on good strong straight stalks above dwarf procumbent foliage. For best effect plant 'Leora' in groups or drifts to the front of a flower border, where it will not receive undue competition from neighbouring plants.

Palmer's White

▷ Raised by Mr Palmer of Northenden well over fifty years ago, this pure white viola is a particularly fine variety. The comparatively large flowers are of perfect proportions, their circular outline being broken only by the most delicate filigree edging. The plant is of dwarf stature and tidy habit, with short sturdy flower stems which provide effective resistance against wind damage. A surface mulch applied around the plant will help to protect the snow-white petals from any disfigurement which might be caused by splashing from heavy rain. This valuable old variety should be propagated each season as an insurance lest it fail to survive the winter.

Gladys Finlay

◁ A tall robust viola with comparatively large and striking flowers which truly compensate in quality for what they may lack in quantity. The flowers are displayed on stout wind-resistant stems. The top two petals are comparable to purple velvet, and the remaining three are white, veined, flushed and margined with violet-blue. A bold rich yellow eye adds an appropriate finishing touch to this fine old variety. The plant has a tendency towards the lax habit of the garden pansy, and for that reason should, for best effect, be grown in groups rather than as an isolated specimen in the flower border.

Buxton Blue

▷ This fine old variety has a neat compact habit, and its medium-sized, short-stemmed flowers are of a clear strong blue with distinct dark indigo central markings, characteristics not unlike those of the fancy or blotched pansy. It is one of the best blue violas. Previous generations have known it as 'Bluestone' or 'Blue Boy', but it is as 'Buxton Blue' that it will be found listed in the specialist catalogues of today. No longer the most vigorous of varieties, it must be cultivated with care.

Rebecca

▷ This particularly fine variety of violetta has been introduced within the last twenty years. The plant has an excellent dwarf compact habit and neat attractive foliage. Exceptional resistance to harsh weather conditions enable it to survive where less robust varieties might fail. The delicately fragrant flowers are exceptionally attractive, having frilled petals of white overlaid with a bold but variable flaking and edging of rich mauve-violet. 'Rebecca' blooms constantly and profusely throughout the summer months, and is a relatively easy variety to propagate from division of its vigorous rootstock, or from cuttings. A good variety to encourage a novice grower.

Buttercup

◁ A good rich yellow variety, possessing all the requirements of an excellent violetta. Originally named 'Rock Orange', it was introduced by D.B.Crane who devoted much of his life, from the early 1890s, to the cultivation and selection of improved varieties of violetta. Crane's son Howard, who shared his father's passion for violas and violettas, subsequently passed plants of this variety to another plantsman, who renamed it 'Buttercup'.

Prince Henry

▷ This small-flowered viola with rich purple, yellow-centred flowers is a direct descendant of the species *V. tricolor*. It is best treated as an annual or biennial, and raised from fresh seed each season. If seed (readily available from seed merchants) is sown in late summer and given winter protection, it will be ready for planting into the open ground in spring. Alternatively, sow in the spring, in which case plants will commence flowering later in the season. As with most seed-raised plants, there may be a certain degree of variation depending upon the quality of the seed obtained.

Admiration

◁ This well-established vigorous variety is of hardy constitution and proven reliability. It possesses all the basic requirements of a thoroughly good viola. The finely shaped rich violet flowers are of good substance and held aloft on stout stems. The plant has a neat compact habit and grows in a tidy and controlled fashion. Even when the long flowering season is ended, its hummock of healthy green foliage serves to enhance the winter flower garden.

V. cornuta 'Tony Venison'

▷ In common with all the many varieties of V. *cornuta*, this is a thoroughly hardy perennial plant, undemanding in its requirements and easy to propagate by division of the mature rootstock. Its two remarkable characteristics are its flowers, the petals of which are irregularly striped and veined blue and white, and its foliage which, although it begins life bright green, gradually, as the season progresses, adopts variegation of yellow. Ultimately the foliage turns totally golden yellow, forming a most attractive and welcome splash of colour to enhance the viola bed throughout the dark days of winter until flowering begins again.

Dawn

◁ This splendid little lemon-yellow violetta is a particularly attractive, long-established variety and was raised by Howard Crane who, together with his father, did more than most to promote the violetta. The flowers, with very slightly frilled petals, blossom profusely for week after week throughout the summer months. The tufted habit and vigorous root system contribute towards making this one of the most satisfactory varieties for vegetative propagation.

Letitia

▷ No collection of violas is complete without consideration having been given to the inclusion of this delightful and unusual variety. The colour of the flowers, best described as pale purple-pink with central markings of a similar deeper richer shade, blends harmoniously with all other varieties, but is sufficiently distinct and unusual to ensure that it will always attract particular attention. The freshly opened flower buds have a richness of colour which fades slightly as the petals become exposed to prolonged sunlight. Self-sown seedlings from 'Letitia' very often retain all the essential characteristics of the parent plant.

Barbara

◁ A splendid bedding viola whose rather coarse and procumbent framework is compensated for by the rich opulence of its flowers which are a most striking combination of warm mauve and rich golden yellow. The top two petals are predominantly mauve, and the remaining three bear varying degrees of golden yellow and mauve combined. 'Barbara' provides a welcome spot of warmth in contrast to the many cooler-coloured violas. It is best planted in groups or drifts so that each plant can intermingle with its neighbour.

Ardross Gem

▷ A true gem, this small but vigorous compact and free-flowering viola has great charm. The upper four petals of the flower are clear bright violet-blue and the bottom petal provides a contrast of rich golden-yellow. The dainty, slightly elongated flowers are of fine texture and are displayed over a neat cushion of rich green foliage. A well grown single plant should provide a fine specimen for the front of the flower border or a moist pocket in the rock garden. It is equally suitable for growing in a pot, tub or trough. Division of the rootstock is a relatively simple method of propagation.

Desdemona

◁ The flowers of 'Desdemona' are amongst the smallest of all hybrid garden violas, being little larger than those of the wild pansy or Heartsease. A mixture of pale sky blue and white, rayed and with a yellow centre, they are borne in great profusion in constant succession throughout the summer. A single plant will spread to 12 in/30 cm or more in diameter, smothered in blossom. This perfect little cottage garden plant is ideally suited to the forefront of the flower border or to being grown in a pot or other container.

Little David

▷ A thoroughly good violetta whose vigour and comparative ease of propagation should ensure that it will be a firm favourite for many years to come. 'Little David' has ivory white flowers with slightly frilled petals held gracefully erect on good strong straight stems over a neat cushion of foliage. Almost certainly closely related to 'Rebecca', with which it shares almost every characteristic except colour, it is a variety to recommend to the novice grower who should have no difficulty cultivating it successfully. It has pronounced fragrance, the admirable characteristic which all violettas ideally should, but sadly do not always, possess.

Myfanwy

◁ This is a charming viola with very pale mauve flowers. The petals have pronounced veining of a richer mauve and are overlaid with a marbling of white. The elongated flowers are little more than 1 in/2.5 cm in width, and are perfectly complemented by the neat compact foliage. 'Myfanwy' belongs to the group of smaller-flowered varieties with true tufted habit – arguably the most satisfactory and irresistible of all the hybrid violas that are now available to gardeners.

Irish Molly

▷ This curious and unusual viola can be confused with no other. It is one of the older established varieties and never fails to attract attention and comment. The exceptional combination of colours is by no means easily described, and the problem is compounded by there being considerable variation from flower to flower within a single plant. The two upper petals are maroon-brown overcast with a hint of violet, the two middle petals might be described as khaki-yellow with a hint of green, and the bottom petal has a greater concentration of yellow. A chocolate-rayed centre completes the picture.

Jackanapes

◁ This distinctive variety was raised and introduced by the influential gardener and garden designer, Gertrude Jekyll (1843-1932), and named, so we are told, after her pet monkey. The plant is of short-jointed, compact, dwarf habit with small neat foliage. The top two petals are of rich undiluted chocolate-brown, and the remaining three are of a contrasting rich yellow, overlaid with chocolate rays. The sharply defined contrast between these two colours ensures that this splendid viola always stands out from the crowd.

Zara

◁ This fine bedding viola has particularly graceful and attractive flowers, with frilled edges to the petals. From an orange centre the primrose-cream petals gradually become increasingly suffused with warm mauve, culminating in a rich mauve outer margin which is especially pronounced on the top two petals. The overall result is a flower of great delicacy and charm in an exquisite combination of colours.

Mauve Haze

▷ A dainty and delicate small-flowered viola of subdued colouring. The petals open ivory white, and as the flower matures, gradually become overlaid with a wash of the palest violet-mauve. Black rays radiate like little whiskers from the rich yellow centre of the flower. 'Mauve Haze' is an appropriate variety for a corner of the flower garden where stronger more strident colours will not be able to outshine its performance. It is a thoroughly good little cottage garden variety. The overall impact of this viola can be enhanced, where space permits, by planting *en masse*. A generous planting of a single variety can very often be dramatically more effective than too varied a selection.

Specialist Nurseries

BRITAIN
Bouts Cottage Nurseries, Bouts Lane, Nr Inkberrow,
Worcs WR7 4HP

Richard G.M. Cawthorne, Lower Daltons Nursery, Swanley Village,
Swanley, Kent BR8 7NU

Hazeldene Nursery, Dean Street, East Farleigh, Maidstone,
Kent ME15 0PS

Elizabeth MacGregor, Ellenbank, Tongland Road,
Kirkcudbright DG6 4UU

AMERICA
Canyon Creek Nursery, 3527 Dry Creek Road, Oroville, CA 95965